cooking classics
asia

cooking classics

asia

A STEP-BY-STEP COOKBOOK

sylvia kang

Marshall Cavendish
Cuisine

The publisher wishes to thank Pyrex Metalware, Visions and
Ekco 123 for the loan of kitchen utensils used in this book.

Editor : Sylvy Soh
Designer : Bernard Go Kwang Meng
Photographers : Kiyoshi Yoshizawa and Liu Hongde, Jambu Studio

Copyright © 2009 Marshall Cavendish International (Asia) Private Limited

Published by Marshall Cavendish Cuisine
An imprint of Marshall Cavendish International
1 New Industrial Road, Singapore 536196

Other Marshall Cavendish Offices:
Marshall Cavendish Ltd. 5th Floor, 32-38 Saffron Hill, London EC1N 8FH, UK • Marshall Cavendish
Corporation. 99 White Plains Road, Tarrytown NY 10591-9001, USA • Marshall Cavendish International
(Thailand) Co Ltd. 253 Asoke, 12th Flr, Sukhumvit 21 Road, Klongtoey Nua, Wattana, Bangkok 10110,
Thailand • Marshall Cavendish (Malaysia) Sdn Bhd, Times Subang, Lot 46, Subang Hi-Tech Industrial
Park, Batu Tiga, 40000 Shah Alam, Selangor Darul Ehsan, Malaysia

Marshall Cavendish is a trademark of Times Publishing Limited

National Library Board Singapore Cataloguing in Publication Data

Kang, Sylvia, 1978-
Asia : a step-by-step cookbook / Sylvia Kang. – Singapore : Marshall Cavendish Cuisine, c2009.
p. cm. – (Cooking classics)
Includes index.
ISBN-13 : 978-981-261-331-8
ISBN-10 : 981-261-331-5

1. Cookery, Asian. I. Title. II. Series: Cooking classics

TX724.5.A1
641.595 -- dc22   OCN262878125

Printed in Singapore by KWF Printing Pte Ltd

contents

introduction

Asia is a vast, multifaceted melting pot of culture and religion. Many cuisines evolved with the influx of migrants, or influence from neighbouring countries. Depending on the cuisine of the country, flavours can be sweet and sour, spicy and delicate, mild and fiery, salty and bland. Over time and in their own way, each dish has been ensconced as representations of their country's cuisine, and hold their position as firm favourites up till today.

Cambodia, Laos, Thailand and Vietnam

Due to the fact that these countries share a similar climate, there are common ingredients that feature in the cuisines. These include chilli, lemon grass, prawn paste, galangal and fish sauce. Thai, Laotian and Cambodian cuisine is vibrantly hot and spicy in varying degrees. In this aspect, Vietnamese cuisine is slightly different. The French occupation of Vietnam resulted in the introduction of bread and pastries into Vietnamese cuisine. These sit side-by-side along indigeneous Vietnamese dishes today, where flavours are kept simple and light, with an emphasis on fresh herbs and vegetables.

China

As one of the oldest cultures in the world, Chinese cuisine has a rich history. Because of its vast climatic, geographic and cultural diversity, the food is always flavourful and colourful. Eating plays a major role in the Chinese way of life, whether in daily living, rituals or festivities. Regardless of the regional variations, all meals consist of either rice, noodles, dumplings, pancakes or rice cakes.

India

As a country with 15 major languages and 1,600 minor dialects, one can only expect the cooking style of India to differ vastly from state to state. Northern India employs a heavy use of nuts, cream, buttermilk and dried fruit in most dishes. Meal staples consist mainly of *naan*, a flatbread, and *biryani*, a spiced rice dish. In the south, the cuisine is mostly vegetarian, as South Indians are predominantly vegans. Coconut-based dishes such as wet curries, chutneys and pickles are commonly served on banana leaves.

Japan

Japanese cuisine is like a form of art; regardless of the dish, there is a strong emphasis on presentation as well as flavour and freshness. The philosophy behind Japanese cuisine lies in its focus on bringing out the natural flavours of each ingredient, with minimal seasoning.

Korea

Where Japanese cuisine is subtle, Korean cuisine is the opposite. With all sorts of seasoning ingredients employed in the preparation of dishes, Korean dishes scream for attention, with their strong flavours and colourful presentation of ingredients. When cooking, a Korean cook will typically aim to feature five colours (red, green, yellow, white and black) in the dish. Ingredients such as garlic, spring onions, chilli, soy bean paste and sesame oil are heavily employed in cooking.

Indonesia

As Indonesia's cuisine is heavily influenced by religion, there are strict rules to follow when it comes to the types of meat and ingredients used in cooking. Indonesian cooking is typically strong and aromatic, due to the spice pastes which are made from blending an array of herbs and spices.

Singapore and Malaysia

As multi-racial countries, the cuisine of Singapore and Malaysia is diverse, unique and complex. Dishes and cooking styles have risen out of the blending of Chinese, Malay and Indian cooking methods and ingredients. Straits Chinese and Eurasian cuisines are perfect examples; as a result of inter-racial marriages, these cuisines feature a plethora of unique dishes from the marriage of various ingredients.

There is a wide variety of Asian cooking techniques. Depending on the nature of the dish, each technique is employed to bring out the best of flavours and textures.

cooking techniques

boiling

This water-based cooking method involves cooking food in boiling water or liquid. Prolonged boiling at a controlled temperature breaks down the food gradually, causing its flavour to be released into the liquid. Soups and stews are always boiled at low temperature for a long period in order to achieve such a result.

blanching

Blanching involves the plunging of meat or fresh vegetables into boiling water for a brief period of time. This is done to enhance the colour of the food, or to prepare the food for the next step of cooking.

braising and stewing

Braising is typified by searing or browning food at high temperature before liquid is added to continue the cooking process. In stewing, food is simmered in a small amount of water or stock over low heat for a long period of time in a covered pot. The slow cooking process helps develop the flavour of the ingredients, and is particularly suitable for tenderising tough cuts of meat.

deep and shallow frying

Frying involves cooking food in oil or fat. In deep-frying, food is entirely submerged in oil. If done at the right temperature and with clean oil, the deep-fried food will not be excessively oily. In shallow frying, the food is only partially submerged in oil or fat.

grilling and baking

Both methods involve direct cooking food using dry heat to cook food. Grilling typically refers to quick cooking over a barbecue fire, in the oven or in a grill pan. Baking is done over a specified period of time by heat conduction in an oven. The dry heat method causes the outer surfaces of dishes such as meats to brown, giving it a delectable crunch and taste while partially sealing in the food's moisture. As minimal oil is required, these methods are preferred for the healthier option they offer.

steaming

In steaming, food is placed in a special steamer basket or container, which is in turn placed over the boiling water. Minimal moisture, flavour or liquid is lost in the cooking process. It is also a healthy way of cooking, as no oil is required, and the shape and texture of the ingredients are maintained.

stir-frying and pan-frying

In stir-fryiing, a small amount of oil is heated in a wok or frying pan, and the food is stir-fried or tossed in a quick, consistent motion until done. Pan-frying involves the even browning of food in a pan, with or without oil.

salads and starters

fruit and vegetable salad with sweet chilli prawn paste
(indonesia) 18

cold prawn, papaya and vermicelli salad
(thailand) 21

tomato and mango jam (india) 22

mushrooms and rice in bean curd pockets
(japan) 25

seafood and kimchi pancake (korea) 26

spiced potato cakes (malaysia) 29

silky egg custard (japan) 30

herb and vegetable omelette (vietnam) 33

fruit and vegetable salad with sweet chilli prawn paste rojak

There are many versions of this popular Asian salad. This Indonesian version features a selection of fresh fruit and vegetables dressed in a sweet, tangy prawn paste dressing. Serves 4

Black prawn paste (*hae ko*) 3 Tbsp

Lemon juice 1 Tbsp

Turnip 100 g (3¹/₂ oz)

Pineapple 100 g (3¹/₂ oz)

Guava 100 g (3¹/₂ oz)

Cucumber 100 g (3¹/₂ oz), sliced into 2.5-cm (1-in) thick rounds

Thai rose apple 1, cut into wedges

Green apple 1

Large red chilli ¹/₂

1 Combine prawn paste and lemon juice in a mixing bowl. Mix well and set aside.

2 Seed chilli by using the sharp tip of the knife to remove as many seeds as possible, then chop into fine bits and set aside.

3 Peel turnip and pineapple. Discard skin, then cut into bite-sized chunks. Slice guava into wedges and remove seeds using a ring cutter. Remove seeds and discard.

4 Using an apple corer, core green apple and slice into wedges. Do this last, so apple does not oxidise and turn brown.

5 Combine all fruit and vegetables in a large bowl and add prawn paste mixture. Toss lightly to mix well and coat ingredients evenly.

6 Dish out and serve immediately.

cold prawn, papaya and vermicelli salad
yam woon sen

Dressed in a piquant lime and fish sauce dressing, this classic Thai salad whets the appetite for the main meal ahead, and is quick and easy to put together. Serves 4

Green bean vermicelli (glass noodles) 150 g (5$^1/_3$ oz), soaked to soften for 5 minutes and drained

King prawns (shrimps) 250 g (9 oz), peeled and deveined

Green papaya 100 g (3$^1/_2$ oz)

Lime juice 4 Tbsp

Fish sauce 2 Tbsp

Seafood stock (see page 112) 4 Tbsp

Garnish

Red chilli 1, seeded and finely sliced into strips

Mint leaves 1 sprig, chopped

Coriander leaves (cilantro) 1 sprig, coarsely chopped

1 Bring a pot of water to the boil. Add vermicelli and cook for about 3 minutes. Remove vermicelli from pot and quickly plunge in a bowl of iced water. Leave to soak and cool for about 10 minutes, then drain well and set aside.

2 In the same pot of boiling water, cook prawns for 5–10 minutes, or until they turn pink. Remove from heat, drain and quickly plunge into a bowl of iced water. Drain well and set aside.

3 Peel papaya and discard skin. Cut into half, remove seeds and finely slice into thin strips.

4 Combine lime juice, fish sauce and stock in a mixing bowl and mix well. Add vermicelli, prawns and papaya strips, then toss lightly to mix well.

5 Garnish with chilli, mint and coriander leaves and serve immediately.

tomato and mango jam chutney

This sweet, tart chutney is the perfect accompaniment to grilled meat or curries. It can also be used as a condiment or spread for sandwiches. Makes about 400 g (14⅓ oz)

Firm and ripe mango 1, about 200 g (7 oz)

Tomatoes 450 g (16 oz)

Red apple 1, cored, peeled and cut into small cubes

Garlic 1 clove, peeled and chopped

Ginger 2.5-cm (1-in) knob, peeled and finely chopped

Red shallots 6, peeled and chopped

Malt vinegar 300 ml (10 fl oz / 1¼ cups)

Black mustard seeds 1 tsp

Brown sugar 100 g (3½ oz)

1   Using a sharp knife, peel mango and cut into 2.5-cm (1-in) pieces. Cut tomatoes into small wedges, then cut them further into small cubes.

2   Place all ingredients except mango and half of vinegar in a large saucepan. Bring mixture to the boil over medium heat, then reduce heat to low and leave to simmer gently for 30 minutes, stirring occasionally. Add remaining vinegar and leave to simmer gently for 20–30 minutes, stirring occasionally, until mixture thickens.

3   Add mango to chutney mixture and leave to cook for another 5 minutes. Remove from heat and leave aside to cool until warm. Scoop chutney into clean, sterilised jars with airtight lids.

4   Serve chutney with meat dishes, or use as a condiment or spread in sandwiches. Store in sterilsed, airtight jars and keep refrigerated. Chutney can keep refrigerated for up to 2 months.

Tip: To sterilise jars, wash jars well, then wipe dry. Preheat oven to 140°C (280°F), then place jars in for 15 minutes.

mushrooms and rice in bean curd pockets
inari sushi

Traditionally, *inari* sushi simply consists of seasoned Japanese rice stuffed into deep-fried bean curd pockets. A trio of mushrooms, braised in a sweet soy seasoning gives this popular Japanese sushi a tasty twist! Serves 4–6

Japanese short-grain rice 200 g (7 oz), washed and well-drained

Water 250 ml (8 fl oz / 1 cup)

Japanese rice vinegar 4 Tbsp

Sugar 1 tsp

Mushroom filling

Hon shimeji mushrooms 100 g (3½ oz)

Shiitake mushrooms 100 g (3½ oz)

Button mushrooms 100 g (3½ oz)

Cooking oil 1 Tbsp

Light soy sauce 1 Tbsp

Oyster sauce 2 Tbsp

Japanese rice wine (*mirin*) 1 Tbsp

Deep-fried bean curd pockets (*abura-age*) 20 pieces

White sesame seeds 1 Tbsp

1   Combine rice and water in a rice cooker to cook. When rice is done, immediately transfer to a large mixing bowl and stir in rice vinegar and sugar. Set aside to cool.

2   Meanwhile, prepare mushrooms. Using a slightly damp cloth, wipe mushroom caps. Trim off the bases of hon shimeji mushrooms and discard. Slice shiitake and button mushrooms thinly.

3   Heat oil in a frying pan over medium heat and fry mushrooms for 2 minutes. Add soy sauce, oyster sauce and rice wine and stir to mix well. Continue to fry until mushrooms are tender, then remove from heat and set aside.

4   Assemble bean curd bags. Stuff bags with 2–3 Tbsp rice, then spoon 1 Tbsp mushrooms on top of rice. Repeat until ingredients are used up.

5   Garnish with white sesame seeds before serving.

seafood and kimchi pancake bu chu jun

This fragrant seafood pancake is a popular appetiser in Korea. The combination of seafood and vegetables lightly fried in a light pancake batter is a guaranteed crowd pleaser at parties! Serves 4

Store-bought Korean pancake mix
150 g (5¹/₃ oz)

Water 300 ml (10 fl oz / 1¹/₄ cups)

Salt to taste

Ground white pepper to taste

Cooking oil 1 tsp

Eggs 3, beaten with salt and pepper to taste

Pancake ingredients

Carrot 60 g (2 oz)

Squid 120 g (4 oz)

Store-bought cabbage kimchi 60 g (2 oz), thinly sliced

Prawns (shrimps) 120 g (4¹/₄ oz), peeled and thinly sliced

Spring onions (scallions) 2, thinly sliced

1   Place pancake mix in a mixing bowl. Gradually add water and stir until a smooth batter is obtained. Season lightly with salt and pepper and set aside.

2   Peel carrot and discard skin, then slice into thin strips and set aside. Prepare squid (see page 88).

3   Heat oil in non-stick pan over medium heat. When pan is hot, pour half of beaten eggs and half of pancake batter into pan at the same time.

4   Evenly place half of carrot, kimchi, squid, prawns and spring onions on batter. Leave to cook for 2 minutes, or until pancake leaves pan easily. Using a spatula, carefully flip pancake to cook on the other side for another 2 minutes. Remove from heat and set aside. Repeat step to make another pancake using remaining ingredients.

5   Slice pancakes into wedges and serve immediately.

Note: Korean pancake mix is available from all major supermarkets with a Korean food section. To get a thin, crisp pancake, ensure pancake mixture and egg are poured into the pan at the same time.

spiced potato cakes bergedel

It is easy to fall in love with these potato cakes. All you need is some fried onions, garlic and carrots to give the already flavourful potato mash an aromatic boost! Serves 4

Potatoes 500 g (1 lb 1½ oz), peeled

Salt 1 tsp

Ground white pepper to taste

Cooking oil as needed

Shallots 8, peeled and finely chopped

Garlic 5 cloves, peeled and finely chopped

Spring onions (scallions) 2, finely chopped

Carrots 100 g (3½ oz), peeled and finely shredded

Eggs 2, about 55 g (2 oz) each, beaten

1 Place potatoes and salt in a large pot. Add enough water to cover potatoes, then bring to the boil for 15 minutes, or until potatoes are fork-tender. Remove from heat and drain well. Place potatoes in a large mixing bowl and set aside.

2 Heat oil in a frying pan over medium heat. Stir-fry shallots and garlic until fragrant and lightly browned. Remove from heat and place on paper towels to drain excess oil.

3 Add shallots, garlic, spring onions and carrots to potatoes. Using a potato masher, mash potatoes until smooth. Using your hands, shape about 2 Tbsp mash into 5-cm (2-in) round, flat patties.

4 Heat enough oil for shallow-frying in a large frying pan over medium-high heat. Dip patties into beaten egg, then gently place into pan. In batches, fry patties for 2–3 minutes on each side until golden brown. Remove from heat and place on paper towesl to drain excess oil.

5 Garnish patties as desired and serve immediately.

silky egg custard chawanmushi

Mixing the eggs with dashi stock helps to bring out the delicate flavour of the eggs. This simple dish can be prepared in less than 15 minutes. Serves 4

Medium-size eggs 4, beaten

Dashi stock (see page 112)
625 ml (20 fl oz / 2¹/₂ cups)

Light soy sauce 1 tsp

Prawns (shrimps) 4 medium, peeled and deveined

Hon shimeji mushrooms 100 g (3¹/₂ oz), caps wiped and ends trimmed

Salmon roe (optional) 4 tsp

1 Combine eggs, dashi stock and soy sauce in a mixing bowl and mix well. Divide prawns and mushrooms equally into 4 heatproof cups or bowls with lids.

2 Pour an equal amount of egg mixture into cups or bowls. Place cups or bowls in a steamer and cover, if using bowls with lids or aluminium foil. Steam over high heat for 3 minutes, then reduce heat to low and steam for another 8 minutes.

3 Remove cups from heat and uncover. If desired, spoon salmon roe on top of custard and serve immediately.

Tip: To check if egg custard is cooked, tilt cup slightly to one side. Egg custard should have a firm texture and not wobble.

herb and vegetable omelette rau trung trang

Banh xeo is a Vietnamese crêpe that is made with coconut milk, rice flour and eggs and stuffed with meat and vegetables. This is a lighter and healthier version of the crêpe, as the coconut milk and rice flour have been omitted. It is no less delicious though! Serves 4

Green or red capsicum (bell pepper) 100 g (3½ oz), sliced

Cooking oil as needed

Bean sprouts 100 g (3½ oz), tailed

Carrot 100 g (3½ oz), thinly sliced

Oyster sauce 1 Tbsp

Fish sauce 1 tsp

Eggs 4, beaten

Spring onions (scallions) 2

Red chilli 1, deseeded and thinly sliced

Mint leaves 1 sprig, chopped

Basil leaves 1 sprig, chopped

Salt to taste

Ground white pepper to taste

1 Prepare capsicum. Remove stem, then cut in half. Remove the white pith and seeds, then slice into thin strips.

2 Heat 1 Tbsp oil in a non-stick frying pan. Add bean sprouts, carrot and capsicum and stir-fry for 2–3 minutes. Add oyster sauce and fish sauce and stir to mix well. Remove from heat and set aside.

3 In a clean frying pan, heat 1 Tbsp oil and pour in half the beaten eggs. Swirl pan so eggs cover the surface of the frying pan evenly.

4 Place half the vegetables and herbs over egg evenly. Leave to cook for 1–2 minutes, or until egg has set. Fold one side of egg over to form an omelette. Gently remove from pan and place on a serving plate. Repeat steps 3 and 4 to make another omelette.

5 Serve immediately.

rice and noodles

pork and yam rice (china) 36

pineapple fried rice (thailand) 39

vegetable hot stone rice (korea) 40

spicy rice vermicelli soup (laos) 43

longevity noodles (china) 44

salmon udon soup (japan) 47

stir-fried rice noodles (thailand) 48

spicy stir-fried egg noodles in a parcel (singapore) 51

pork and yam rice zhu rou yu tou fan

The simplicity of this fragrant rice dish belies its deliciousness. Cook a big potful for the family, as it is good enough to be a one-dish meal! **Serves 4**

Wood ear fungus 15 g (¹/₂ oz)

Yam 200 g (7 oz), cut into large cubes

Lean pork 250 g (9 oz)

Corn flour (cornstarch) 1 Tbsp

Cooking oil as needed

Garlic 4 cloves, peeled and chopped

Dried prawns (shrimps) 2 Tbsp

Long-grain rice or brown (unpolished) rice 375 g (13 oz), washed and drained

Water or chicken stock (see page 112) 450 ml (15 fl oz / 1⁴/₅ cups)

Seasoning

Oyster sauce 2 Tbsp

Dark soy sauce 2 tsp

Light soy sauce 2 tsp

Water 2 Tbsp

Sesame oil 1¹/₂ Tbsp

1 Soak fungus in a bowl of hot water for about 30 minutes or until soft. Drain and slice thinly and set aside.

2 Peel yam and discard skin. Slice into wedges, then cut further into 1-cm (¹/₂-in) thick cubes. Set aside.

3 Slice pork thinly and place in a bowl. Add corn flour and coat pork slices evenly.

4 Heat enough oil for shallow-frying in a frying pan over medium heat. Fry yam pieces until lightly browned, then remove from pan and set aside.

5 Using the same pan, heat 3 Tbsp oil over medium heat. Fry garlic and dried prawns until fragrant, then add pork and stir-fry for 5 minutes or until pork is well cooked. Add fungus, yam and seasoning ingredients. Stir to mix well. Bring mixture to the boil, then remove from heat.

6 Place rice in a rice cooker. Add water and yam and pork mixture and mix well so that ingredients are evenly distributed. Cook rice until tender.

7 Garnish as desired and serve immediately.

pineapple fried rice kao pad sap pa rod

This dish is a perennial favourite in the realm of Thai rice dishes, and is quick and easy to whip up! Serves 4

Whole pineapple 1, about 600 g
(1 lb 5¹/₃ oz)

Cooking oil 3 Tbsp

Shallots 3, peeled and sliced

Store-bought red curry paste 2 tsp

Cooked long-grain rice 450–500 g
(16–1 lb 1¹/₂ oz), chilled

Yellow curry powder, 1 tsp

Raisins 30 g (1 oz)

Garnish

Red chilli 1, seeded and cut into strips

Store-bought chicken or pork floss 2 Tbsp

Coriander (cilantro) leaves a handful

1 Cut off top and bottom of pineapple, then halve it vertically. Hollow out both halves by scooping out the flesh. Dice flesh into 2.5-cm (1-in) pieces and set aside. Reserve hollowed pineapple halves to use as serving containers.

2 Heat oil in a frying pan over medium heat. Stir-fry shallots and red curry paste for about 10 minutes or until fragrant.

3 Add rice and curry powder and stir to mix well. Use your spatula to break up any clumps in rice. Stir-fry for 5–7 minutes or until rice is heated through. Add pineapple cubes and raisins, then toss lightly to mix well. Remove from heat and transfer rice to pineapple shell container.

4 Garnish with chilli and chicken or pork floss and serve immediately.

Note: Chilled rice is appropriate for fried rice dishes. Unlike warm, freshly cooked rice, it does not become mushy during the cooking process, allowing every grain to be evenly coated with the seasoning.

vegetable hot stone rice bibim bap

This vegetarian version of a well-loved Korean rice dish is not only aesthetically pleasing, but is healthy and tasty as well. Serves 4

Bean sprouts 100 g (3½ oz), tailed

Carrot 100 g (3½ oz), peeled

Green and yellow courgettes (zucchinis) 100 g (3½ oz) each

Spring onions (scallions) 2 sprigs

Shiitake mushrooms 100 g (3½ oz)

Cooking oil as needed

Garlic 5 cloves, peeled and finely chopped

Sesame oil 2 tsp

Salt 2 tsp

Water 2 Tbsp

Cooked short-grain rice 450 g (16 oz)

Store-bought cabbage kimchi 100 g (3½ oz), cut into smaller pieces if pieces are too large

Eggs 4

White sesame seeds 1 tsp

Korean chilli paste 4 Tbsp

1   Prepare vegetables. Cut carrot, courgettes and spring onions into strips of 5-cm (2-in) lengths. Slice mushrooms thinly.

2   Heat 1 Tbsp cooking oil in a frying pan over medium heat. Fry carrots for 1–2 minutes, then add mushrooms, courgettes, spring onions, garlic, sesame oil, salt and water. Stir to mix well and cook for another 2 minutes. Remove from heat and set aside.

3   Heat four lightly oiled stone bowls on a stove over high heat. Divide rice among equally among hot bowls, then arrange equal amounts of stir-fried vegetables and kimchi in neat sections on top of rice. Leave a small space in centre of rice for a fried egg. Remove from stove and set aside.

4   Heat 2 Tbsp oil in a clean frying pan over medium heat. Crack eggs, into pan and cook them sunny-side-up style. Use more oil, if necessary. Carefully slide eggs into the centre of rice without breaking the yoik. If preferred, place eggs on separate side plates .

5   Garnish rice with sesame seeds and serve immediately, with chilli paste on the side.

spicy rice vermicelli soup khao pun nam jio

This Laotian noodle soup features the rich, smoky flavours of pork bone and roasted vegetables. Fresh herbs like basil provide a refreshing lift to the rich flavours, making this perfect for a light lunch. **Serves 4**

Shallots 4, left unpeeled

Garlic 3 cloves, left unpeeled

Red chillies 2

Galangal 25 g ($^3/_4$ oz)

French beans 125 g ($4^1/_4$ oz), thinly sliced

Pork loin 300 g (11 oz)

Pork bones 500 g (1 lb $1^1/_2$ oz)

Water 1.5 litres (48 fl oz / 6 cups)

Kaffir lime leaves 3

Salt 1 tsp

Thin rice vermicelli 250 g (9 oz), rinsed with hot water, then soaked in cold water

Cabbage 120 g ($4^1/_4$ oz), thinly sliced

Bean sprouts 120 g ($4^1/_4$ oz), tailed

Condiments

Limes 2, halved

Red chilli 1, thinly sliced

Chilli powder 2 tsp

Sweet basil leaves a handful

Coriander leaves (cilantro) a handful

1 Roast shallots, garlic and chillies over an open flame until slightly charred. Set aside.

2 Peel and slice galangal into 5 thin slices. Cut French beans thinly on the diagonal.

3 Place pork, pork bones, water, galangal, kaffir lime leaves, salt and roasted vegetables into a large pot and bring to a boil over high heat. When mixture boils, reduce heat to low and leave to simmer for 45 minutes or until meat is tender. Remove pork and place on a chopping board. Slice thinly and set aside.

4 Strain stock into a clean pot. Return to stove and keep warm until use.

5 Divide vermicelli, cabbage, french beans, bean sprouts and sliced pork among 4 serving bowls. Ladle hot stock over, top with condiments and serve immediately.

longevity noodles chang shou mian

Longevity noodles are traditionally served by Chinese families during the birthday of a family member. My grandmother used to remind us not to bite through the noodles so that the person whose birthday was being celebrated would enjoy longevity! **Serves 4**

Sesame oil 2 Tbsp

Shallots 6, peeled and thinly sliced

Garlic 4 cloves, peeled and finely chopped

Seafood stock (see page 112) 2 litres (64 fl oz / 8 cups)

Prawns (shrimps) 300 g (11 oz), peeled and deveined, heads left intact

Chinese cabbage (*bak choy*) 200 g (7 oz)

Wheat flour vermicelli 180 g (6¹/₂ oz), rinsed and drained

1 Heat oil in a frying pan over medium heat. Fry shallots and garlic until crisp and fragrant. Divide into 2 portions and set aside.

2 Cut off the ends of the cabbage bunches and discard. Rinse leaves and drain well. Set aside.

3 Place 1 portion of fried shallots and garlic into a pot. Add stock and bring to the boil over high heat. Add prawns and cabbage and cook for 3–5 minutes or until prawns are cooked. Drain prawns and cabbage and set aside.

4 Add vermicelli to stock and cook for 1–2 minutes. Remove from heat, then divide among prepared serving bowls.

5 Arrange prawns, cabbage, fried shallots and garlic on top of noodles. Drizzle with a little sesame oil and serve immediately.

Tip: Cook this dish just before serving, as wheat flour vermicelli tends to absorb the stock very quickly. Even leaving the dish stand for less than 5 minutes will cause the vermicelli to become soggy.

salmon udon soup sake udon

Udon noodle soup is characterised by its mild, dashi-based stock. This dish can be prepared under 30 minutes, and is perfect for a light lunch. **Serves 4**

Dashi stock (see page 112) 1.5 litres
  (48 fl oz / 6 cups)

Salmon bones 300 g (11 oz)

Salmon fillet 300 g (11 oz)

Snow peas 160 g (5²/₃ oz)

Udon noodles 600 g (1 lb 5¹/₃ oz),
  rinsed with hot water

Finely shredded seaweed (*nori*) 20 g (²/₃ oz)

1 Combine dashi stock and salmon bones in a large pot. Bring to the boil over medium heat, then reduce heat a little and leave to simmer gently for 15 minutes before removing bones.

2 Meanwhile, slice salmon into 0.5-cm (¹/₄-in) thick slices and set aside.

3 Prepare snow peas. Using a knife, gently peel away the stringy fibre along the length of the pea, starting from the stem end. Discard fibre.

4 Place snow peas and salmon into stock and leave to cook for 3 minutes, or until salmon is cooked.

5 Rinse udon noodles in hot water and divide among 4 serving bowls. Ladle stock over noodles, then arrange snow peas and salmon on top. Garnish with seaweed and serve immediately.

stir-fried rice noodles pad thai

Pad thai is a popular Thai street food dish. Full of flavour, colour and texture, it will make a delicious one-dish meal! Serves 4

Cooking oil 3 Tbsp

Onion 55 g (2 oz), peeled and thinly sliced

Dried prawns (shrimps) 3 Tbsp, soaked in hot water for 10 minutes and drained

Firm bean curd 100 g (3½ oz), cut into 2.5-cm (1-in) pieces

Eggs 2, beaten

Thai dried stick noodles 250 g (9 oz), soaked in warm water to soften and drained

Bean sprouts 100 g (3½ oz), tailed

Garlic chives 85 g (3 oz), cut into 3-cm (1½-in) lengths

Seasoning

Tamarind pulp 1 Tbsp

Warm water 4 Tbsp

Fish sauce 2 Tbsp

Oyster sauce 2 Tbsp

Brown sugar 1 tsp

Condiments

Chilli flakes to taste

Crushed unsalted peanuts 4 tsp

Lime 1, cut into wedges

1 Combine tamarind pulp with warm water in a mixing bowl and mix well. If necessary, use your fingers to knead and dissolve pulp. Strain and discard fibre and seeds. Set aside.

2 Heat oil in large wok over medium heat. Stir-fry onion and dried prawns until fragrant, then add bean curd and stir-fry for 3–5 minutes until lightly browned.

3 Push ingredients to one side of wok and pour in beaten egg. Leave egg to cook for about 2 minutes, then use your spatula to break it up into small pieces.

4 Add noodles, bean sprouts and chives and stir-fry for 3 minutes over high heat. Add tamarind juice and other seasoning ingredients. Toss gently to mix well and remove from heat.

5 Sprinkle chilli flakes and peanuts over noodles and place lime wedges on the side. Serve immediately.

spicy stir-fried egg noodles in a parcel
mee goreng pattaya

Take a moment to enjoy the first whiff of the aromatic sambal when you slice open the omelette parcel to indulge in the deliciously spicy noodles! **Serves 4**

Cooking oil 3 Tbsp

Shallots 3, peeled and thinly sliced

Garlic 2 cloves, peeled and finely chopped

Sambal *belacan* **(see page 113)** 4 Tbsp

Fish cake 150 g ($5^1/_3$ oz), finely sliced

Yellow egg noodles 400 g ($14^1/_3$ oz), rinsed and drained

Chinese flowering cabbage (*chye sim*) 200 g (7 oz), cut into 5-cm (2-in) lengths

Eggs 4, beaten with salt and ground white pepper

Seasoning

Sweet chilli sauce 2 Tbsp

Dark soy sauce 1 Tbsp

Water 4 Tbsp

1　Heat 2 Tbsp oil in a wok over medium heat. Add shallots and garlic and stir-fry until fragrant. Add sambal *belacan* and stir-fry for 3 minutes, then add fish cake. Add noodles, vegetables and seasoning ingredients. Stir-fry for 3–5 minutes, tossing gently to mix well. Dish out and set aside.

2　Heat remaining oil in a large, flat frying pan over medium heat. Add beaten eggs and swirl pan so eggs coat the base. When egg has cooked and set, gently place a round heap of noodles onto centre of omelette. Fold the sides of the omelette up to enclose noodles.

3　Place a serving plate over noodle parcel and carefully turn the parcel onto the plate.

4　Cut parcel open to reveal the noodles. Garnish as desired and serve immediately.

meat and poultry

braised chicken in vinegar and soy sauce
(the philippines) 54

stir-fried red curry chicken (thailand) 57

paper-wrapped chicken with mushrooms (china) 58

ginseng chicken soup (korea) 61

braised pork in dark soy sauce (china) 62

pumpkin pork rib soup (china) 65

rice paper pork parcels (vietnam) 66

grilled teriyaki beef (japan) 69

stir-fried spicy beef (cambodia) 70

grilled lamb and mint kebabs (india) 73

braised chicken in vinegar and soy sauce
adobo manok

This is a popular dish in the Philippines. Chicken is simmered in vinegar and soy sauce until tender. A perfect dish to go with rice. **Serves 4**

Onion 1, peeled

Cooking oil 3 Tbsp

Chicken thigh 4

Garlic 2 cloves, peeled and chopped

White (distilled) vinegar 3 Tbsp

Light soy sauce 5 Tbsp

Sugar 1 tsp

Ground black pepper ½ tsp

Bay leaf 1

Water 4 Tbsp

1   Cut onion into quarters, then cut further into thick slices.

2   Heat oil over medium heat. Place chicken thighs skin side down in pan and fry for 5–8 minutes on each side, or until golden brown. Remove from pan and set aside.

3   In the same pan, stir-fry onion and garlic for 5 minutes, or until fragrant.

4   Add remaining ingredients to pan and mix well. Return chicken to pan, then bring mixture to the boil over high heat. Reduce heat to low, cover and simmer for 30–40 minutes, or until chicken is tender.

5   Dish out and serve hot, with steamed white rice.

stir-fried red curry chicken pad prik kang

As compared to traditional versions of red curry, which are rich in coconut milk, this recipe uses a comparatively small amount of coconut milk, but is just as tasty! Serves 4

Dried prawns (shrimps) 2 tsp, soaked in
warm water for 10 minutes and drained

Kaffir lime leaves 3

Cooking oil 2 Tbsp

Red curry paste (see page 113) 2 Tbsp

Chicken fillet 450 g (16 oz), cut into cubes

Corn flour (cornstarch) 2 Tbsp

Fish sauce 1 Tbsp

Coconut milk 4 Tbsp

Sugar 1/2 tsp

Water 3 Tbsp

1   Using a chef's knife, chop dried prawns up finely. Do this by keeping the tip of the knife on the chopping board with one hand and moving the knife up and down with the other hand.

2   Using a small knife, cut out the tough centre vein from the kaffir lime leaves and discard. Finely slice one leaf into small strips and set aside a little for garnishing.

3   Heat 2 Tbsp oil in a frying pan over medium heat. Add red curry paste and dried prawns and stir-fry for about 5 minutes until fragrant.

4   Coat chicken cubes with corn flour just before adding to pan. Stir-fry for 5 minutes until chicken is cooked. Add fish sauce, coconut milk, sugar, water and kaffir lime leaves and stir-fry for 2 minutes.

5   Dish out and garnish with finely sliced kaffir lime leaf. Serve immediately.

paper-wrapped chicken with mushrooms
zhi bao ji

Steaming rather than deep-frying this popular Cantonese dish results in juicy and flavourful chicken, as it absorbs the seasoning while cooking in its own juices. Serves 4

Chicken drumsticks 4, large

Dried Chinese mushrooms 6, soaked in water to soften, then halved

Chinese sausage 85 g (3 oz), thinly sliced

Spring onions (scallions) 2, cut into 6-cm (2$\frac{1}{2}$-in) lengths

Parchment paper 4 square sheets, each 20 x 20 cm (8 x 8-in)

Corn flour (cornstarch) 1 Tbsp

Marinade

Oyster sauce 3 Tbsp

Dark soy sauce 1 Tbsp

Light soy sauce 1 tsp

Sesame oil 1 Tbsp

1 Using a sharp knife, score drumsticks by making 2–3 diagonal cuts on chicken drumsticks.

2 Combine ingredients for marinade in a bowl. Add chicken and mushrooms and mix well. Cover, refrigerate and marinate for at least 1 hour.

3 Lay a sheet of parchment paper on a flat work surface. Place 1 chicken drumstick and some Chinese mushrooms, Chinese sausage and spring onion on the centre of the parchment paper. Spoon 1 Tbsp marinade over.

4 Fold 2 opposite sides of paper over chicken, then twist open ends to seal. Repeat to make another 3 parcels. Place parcels in a steamer and steam for 20–30 minutes.

5 Unwrap parcels just before serving.

Note: Aluminium foil can be used in place of parchment paper for wrapping ingredients. Seal parcels with a double layer of foil to ensure that they are sealed tightly.

ginseng chicken soup samgaetahng

This Korean chicken dish is warming and nutritious, due to the use of ginseng, a herb which is renowned for its restorative properties. Serves 4

Whole chicken 1, medium

Salt to taste

Glutinous (sticky) rice 85 g (3 oz), rinsed and drained

Ginseng root 2 pieces

Fresh gingko nuts 8, shelled, peeled and bitter shoots removed, or use canned gingko nuts

Garlic 3 cloves, rinsed

Water 2 litres (64 fl oz / 8 cups)

Red dates 5, pitted

Ground white pepper to taste

1 Clean chicken and discard organs. Cut off and discard head, feet, wing tips and neck. Rub the skin and cavity with salt, then rinse with water thoroughly.

2 Stuff chicken with rice, ginseng, gingko nuts and garlic into the cavity of chicken. Bind legs using kitchen string to seal cavity and keep stuffing in.

3 Place chicken in a large pot, add water and bring to the boil over high heat. Skim off any impurities that rise to the surface and reduce heat to low. Cover and leave to simmer for 45 minutes.

4 Add red dates and pepper. Continue to simmer gently for another 30–40 minutes, or until chicken is tender.

5 Carefully remove kitchen string with a knife or pair of scissors. Dish out and serve hot.

Note: An easy way to prepare fresh gingko nuts is to break open the shells gently with a small hammer. Soak in hot water for 5 minutes so that the skin can be peeled easily.

braised pork in dark soy sauce lu rou

This classic Hokkien recipe, which was passed down to me by my grandmother, features pork in a rich, aromatic dark soy sauce marinade, braised until meltingly tender. **Serves 4**

Pork belly 800 g (1³/₄ lb)

Cooking oil 2 Tbsp

Water 85 ml (2¹/₂ fl oz / ¹/₃ cup)

Steamed Chinese buns 8–10

Marinade

Dark soy sauce 4 Tbsp

Light soy sauce 1¹/₂ Tbsp

Star anise 1

Cinnamon sticks 2

Sugar 2 tsp

Cloves 5

Garlic 10 cloves

1   Combine ingredients for marinade in a large bowl. Add pork and mix well. Cover, refrigerate and marinate for at least 1 hour.

2   Heat oil in a large pot over high heat. Sear pork for 3 minutes, or until evenly browned. Add marinade and water, then cover and leave to cook for 30 minutes, stirring occasionally. Reduce heat to low, then leave to simmer for another 40–50 minutes, or until meat is tender. If sauce starts to dry up, add a little water.

3   Slice pork thickly. Serve with Chinese steamed buns, or plain white rice.

Note: For a healthier alternative, use pork loin instead of pork belly.

pumpkin pork rib soup nan gua pai gu tang

Choose a sweet-fleshed pumpkin to get the best out of this flavourful soup. Serves 4

Pumpkin 400 g (14$^{1}/_{3}$ oz)

Pork ribs 500 g (1 lb 1$^{1}/_{3}$ oz)

Water 1 litre (32 fl oz / 4 cups)

Onion 1, peeled and cut into quarters

Garlic 4 cloves

Light soy sauce 1 tsp

1   Cut pumpkin into quarters. Scrape out seeds and fibre using a spoon.
    Cut skin from pumpkin, then cut into large chunks.

2   Place pork ribs in a large bowl and pour boiling water over to scald ribs
    to remove impurities. Drain well, then transfer to a large pot. Add water,
    onion and garlic then bring to the boil over high heat. Add pumpkin,
    then reduce heat and leave to simmer for about 1 hour, or until pork ribs
    are tender.

3   Dish out and serve immediately.

Note: If desired, serve soup with thinly sliced red chillies and dark soy
sauce as a condiment on the side.

rice paper pork parcels thit nuong la lot

These tasty Vietnamese pork parcels will be a hit at parties. Makes about 10 parcels

Lean minced pork 500 g (1 lb 1½ oz)

Onion 1, peeled and chopped

Garlic 3 cloves, peeled and chopped

Basil leaves 2 sprigs, half portion finely chopped and remaining portion left whole

Fish sauce 2 tsp

Sugar 1 tsp

Ground black pepper ¼ tsp

Vietnamese rice paper 10 sheets

Coriander leaves (cilantro) a few sprigs

Cooking oil 4–5 Tbsp

Condiment

Vietnamese sweet chilli sauce

1 Combine pork, onion, garlic, chopped basil leaves, fish sauce, sugar and pepper in a large bowl and mix well. Set aside.

2 Soak rice paper sheets, one at a time in a shallow bowl of warm water for about 1 minute or until soft. Carefully remove and place on a moist, clean cloth to absorb excess water.

3 Place rice paper sheet on a flat work surface. In the centre, place a basil leaf, coriander leaf and 1 heaped Tbsp pork filling. Flatten filling with a spoon and fold 2 opposite sides of rice paper towards the centre over filling. Fold remaining 2 sides over to make a parcel. Repeat steps 2–3 until ingredients are used up.

4 Heat oil in a non-stick frying pan over medium heat. Add parcels and pan-fry for about 3–5 minutes on each side, or until golden brown.

5 Serve warm with Vietnamese sweet chilli sauce.

grilled teriyaki beef gyu teriyaki

Tender, succulent beef is seasoned with a simple teriyaki-based sauce that goes perfectly with the natural sweetness and flavour of the meat. Serves 4

Japanese cucumber 1

Carrot 1

Cooking oil 2 Tbsp

Ribeye steak 500 g (1 lb 1^1/$_2$ oz)

Teriyaki sauce

Brown onion ^{1}/$_2$, peeled and sliced

Mirin 3 Tbsp

Light soy sauce 3 Tbsp

Sugar 1^1/$_2$ Tbsp

1   Heat 1 Tbsp oil in a small saucepan over medium heat. Stir-fry onion until brown and soft. Add mirin, soy sauce and sugar. Reduce heat and simmer until sauce is reduced to a thick consistency. Remove from heat and set aside.

2   Heat a grill pan over medium heat and brush with a little oil. Place steak on pan and brush with teriyaki sauce. Grill for 5–10 minutes on each side, until steak is cooked to desired doneness.

3   Peel cucumber and carrot. Discard skin, then shred into thin strips using a vegetable peeler.

4   Serve beef immediately, with shredded cucumber and carrot slices on the side.

stir-fried spicy beef chha sakh krceung

This quick, easy stir-fry features fresh herbs, and spices add an irresistable aroma and flavour to the beef. Serves 4

Cooking oil 2 Tbsp

Marbled beef steak 4, about 200 g (7 oz) per steak, finely sliced

Spice paste

Lemon grass 2 stalks

Galangal 2 slices

Turmeric 2 slices

Garlic 3 cloves, peeled

Red chilli 1, seeded

Seasoning

Sugar 1 tsp

Salt ½ tsp

Oyster sauce 2 tsp

Fish sauce 1 tsp

1   Peel hard outer leaves from lemon grass, then trim green portion and base and discard.

2   Chop lemon grass coarsely and place in a blender. Add galangal, turmeric, garlic and chilli, then blend until fine. Set aside.

3   Heat oil in a frying pan over medium heat. Stir-fry beef for 3 minutes. Add blended spice paste. Stir to mix well and stir-fry for 3 minutes, or until fragrant. Add seasoning ingredients and mix well before removing from heat. Meat should be tender.

4   Dish out and serve immediately.

grilled lamb and mint kebabs kofta

Simply seasoned with mint leaves, lime and pepper, these kebabs are great as finger food for serving at outdoor parties or barbecues. **Serves 4**

Lean minced lamb 500 g (1 lb 1½ oz)

Red capsicum (bell pepper) 55 g (2 oz) finely chopped

Shallots 5, peeled and finely chopped

Mint leaves 1 sprig, finely chopped

Coarsely ground black pepper ½ tsp

Canola oil 3 Tbsp

Lime juice 1 Tbsp

Mint yoghurt sauce

Plain natural yoghurt 5 Tbsp

Cucumber 55 g (2 oz), finely chopped

Mint leaves 6, finely chopped

Garnish

Lime ½

Mint leaves a handful

1 Combine ingredients for mint yoghurt sauce in a mixing bowl and mix well. Refrigerate until needed.

2 Combine remaining ingredients in a mixing bowl and mix well.

3 Shape 1½ Tbsp of meat mixture into approximately 7-cm (3-in) sausages. Skewer with bamboo or metal skewers.

4 Heat a grill pan over high heat and brush with a little oil. Grill kebabs for 5–8 minutes, turning over occasionally to cook evenly.

5 Serve immediately, with mint yoghurt sauce, lime and mint leaves on the side.

Note: Soak bamboo skewers in water for about 20 minutes sbefore use to prevent them from burning while grilling.

fish and seafood

steamed cod fillet with crispy toppings (china) 76

fish fillet with lemon-orange glace (thailand) 79

spicy coconut fishcake in banana leaves (malaysia) 80

grilled mackerel (korea) 83

prawn and pineapple tamarind curry (singapore) 84

grilled prawn on sugar cane skewers (vietnam) 87

stir-fried squid with chilli paste (malaysia) 88

creamy miso seafood claypot stew (japan) 91

steamed cod fillet with crispy toppings
zhen xue yu

All it takes is a little stir-fried pickled turnip, garlic and shallots to make an already flavourful steamed cod fillet even tastier. **Serves 4**

Cooking oil 2 Tbsp

Cod fillets 4

Ginger 3 slices, peeled and cut into fine strips

Crispy toppings

Shallots 3, peeled and finely chopped

Garlic 3 cloves, peeled and finely chopped

Chopped preserved turnip 3 Tbsp

Seasoning

Light soy sauce 2 tsp

Sesame oil 1 tsp

Sugar 1/4 tsp

Water 3 Tbsp

1 Prepare crispy topping. Heat oil in a frying pan over medium heat. Stir-fry shallots, garlic and pickled radish until fragrant and crisp. Remove from heat and set aside.

2 Place fish on a heatproof plate and top with ginger. Set aside.

3 Combine ingredients for seasoning and mix well. Pour over fish, then place fish in a steamer and steam for 10–12 minutes, or until fish is cooked.

4 Transfer fish, together with steaming juices onto a serving plate. Top with crispy toppings and garnish as desired.

Note: The ingredients for crispy toppings can also be prepared in a microwave oven. Place ingredients in a microwave-safe bowl and stir in 2 Tbsp oil. Cover and cook on High for 1–2 minutes.

fish fillet with lemon-orange glacé
pla tod sauce manao

A zesty glacé made from fresh orange and lemon gives this crispy fish fillet instant zing! **Serves 4**

Red snapper fillets 4

Plain (all-purpose) flour 2 Tbsp

Salt 1 tsp

Ground white pepper ½ tsp

Cooking oil for deep-frying

Red chilli 1, seeds removed and finely chopped

Glacé

Orange 1

Lemon ½

Corn flour (cornstarch) 2 tsp

Sugar 1 tsp

Water 3 Tbsp

1 Prepare glacé. Grate orange and lemon for zest. Alternatively, use a vegetable peeler and cut away the white pith, then slice zest into fine strips. Squeeze orange and lemon to extract juice and strain to remove seeds. Set aside.

2 Pat dry fish fillets with paper towels. Mix flour, salt and pepper and sprinkle mixture over fish to coat lightly.

3 Heat oil for deep-frying in a frying pan over medium heat. Carefully lower in fillets and deep-fry for 8–10 minutes until golden brown. Remove from heat and place on paper towels to drain off excess oil.

4 Combine all ingredients for glacé in a small saucepan. Bring to the boil, then lower heat and leave to simmer until reduced to a thick consistency.

5 Arrange fish fillets on a serving plate. Pour glacé over just before serving. Garnish with chopped red chilli and serve immediately.

spicy coconut fishcake in banana leaves
otah-otah

This popular Malay dish consists of fish that is blended with fragrant herbs and spices, then wrapped in banana leaves and baked to perfection. Serves 4

Fish fillet (Spanish mackerel) 300 g (11 oz), remove skin and chopped into cubes

Corn flour (cornstarch) 1 Tbsp

Salt ½ tsp

Ground white pepper 3 dashes

Banana leaf 1

Spice paste

Kaffir lime leaves 6, centre vein removed and thinly sliced

Lime juice 1 Tbsp

Sambal *belacan* (see page 113) 4 Tbsp

Coconut milk or evaporated milk 90 ml (3 fl oz / ³⁄₈ cup)

Sugar 1 tsp

Lemon grass 2 stalks, tough outer leaves removed, ends trimmed and sliced

Curry powder 1 tsp

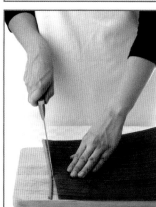

1   Preheat oven to 180°C (350°F). Wrap a baking tray with aluminium foil.

2   Using a sharp knife, cut into fish at a 45° angle, stopping just before the skin. Cut skin away from fish.

3   Place fish in a mixing bowl, then season with corn flour, salt and pepper. Transfer fish to a blender, then add ingredients for spice paste and blend until smooth. Set aside.

4   Cut out tough centre vein from banana leaf, then cut leaf into 2 large squares. Scoop half of fish paste and place in the centre of one banana leaf square. Use a spoon to level and flatten paste. Fold 2 opposite sides of leaf over paste, then secure open ends with toothpicks. Repeat to make another parcel.

5   Place banana leaf parcels onto prepared baking tray. Bake for 15–20 minutes, or until fish cake is firm and cooked.

6   Unwrap parcels just before serving. Garnish as desired and serve.

Note: Serve fish cake as a snack, or as part of a main meal. Any other firm fleshed oily fish is suitable for this dish. If banana leaves are unavailable, use aluminium foil instead.

grilled mackerel ggongchi gui

Grilling is one of the best ways to ensure a fish is cooked in its natural omega oils and juices. All it needs is a simple seasoning to get a moist and tender fish with slightly crisp skin. Serves 4

Mackerel (*saba*) 1, about 20-cm (8-in)
   in length

Sea salt 2 tsp

Canola oil 1 tsp

Sesame oil 2 tsp

Lemon 1, cut into wedges

1 Preheat oven to 180°C (350°F). Wrap a baking tray with aluminium foil.

2 Clean and gut fish, then make 3–4 diagonal cuts on each side of fish.
   Place fish on prepared baking tray. Rub both sides of fish with salt,
   being careful to season slits made in fish as well.

3 Mix canola and sesame oil in a small bowl. Squeeze the juice from
   a lemon wedge into oil and stir. Pour over fish.

4 Place fish in oven and grill for about 15–20 minutes, or until fish exudes
   clear juices and flesh flakes easily.

5 Remove from heat and transfer to a serving plate. Garnish as desired and
   serve immediately, with remaining lemon wedges.

Note: If using small mackerel, bake for less than 15 minutes.

prawn and pineapple tamarind curry
udang pedas nanas

Cooked in fresh pineapple juice and a tamarind-curry spice paste, this refreshing dish of curried prawns will whet any appetite! **Serves 4**

Large prawns (shrimps)
600 g (1 lb 5^1/$_3$ oz)

Pineapple 1 small, about 500 g
(1 lb 1^1/$_2$ oz)

Tamarind pulp 2 Tbsp, mixed with
180 ml (6 fl oz / ^{3}/$_4$ cup) warm water
and strained

Cooking oil 2 Tbsp

Salt to taste

Seafood stock (see page 112) or water
100 ml (3^1/$_3$ fl oz)

Spice paste

Shallots 10, peeled and chopped

Red chillies 5, seeds removed and sliced

Tumeric 15 g (^{1}/$_2$ oz)

Dried prawn (shrimp) paste (*belacan*)
1 tsp

Lemon grass 2 stalks, tough outer layer
removed, ends trimmed and sliced

1. Carefully peel shell from prawns, leaving head and tails intact. Using a small sharp knife, make a slit down the back of prawn, then remove the vein. Rinse prawns, drain and set aside.

2. Peel pineapple and cut in half. Remove core, then cut pineapple flesh into cubes. Place half of cubes in a blender and blend into a purée. Strain through a fine mesh sieve to remove fibre, using a spoon to push purée through the sieve. This should yield about 85 ml (2^1/$_2$ fl oz / ^{1}/$_3$ cup) juice. Set aside.

3. Prepare spice paste. Using a small knife, carefully peel skin from turmeric and slice finely. Place remaining ingredients in a blender and blend into a fine paste.

4. Heat oil in large saucepan over medium heat. Fry spice paste for about 10 minutes until fragrant. Add salt, tamarind juice, pineapple juice, stock or water and pineapple cubes. Stir to mix well, then increase heat and bring mixture to the boil.

5. Add prawns and leave to cook for 8–10 minutes, until prawns turn pink and are cooked. Remove from heat, then dish out and serve.

grilled prawns on sugar cane skewers
cha tom

Marinated in an aromatic concoction of mint, garlic, fish sauce and lime juice, these delicious prawn skewers are fantastic appetisers! Serves 4

Sugar cane 2 sticks,
  each 10-cm (4-in) long

Large prawns (shrimps)
  600 g (1lb 5^1/$_3$ oz), about 12 prawns,
  peeled and deveined

Lettuce leaves for garnish

Marinade

Garlic 6 cloves, peeled and sliced

Spring onions (scallions) 2, sliced

Mint leaves 1 sprig, sliced

Red chilli 1, seeds removed and sliced

Brown sugar 1 tsp

Fish sauce 1 Tbsp

Lime juice 1^1/$_2$ Tbsp

Canola oil 2 Tbsp

1 Make sugar cane skewers. Using a sharp knife, carefully cut off skin. Cut sugar cane into 12 thin sticks. Diagonally trim sticks on one end to create a sharp point.

2 Combine ingredients for marinade in a blender and blend into a fine paste. Place prawns in a mixing bowl, then pour marinade over prawns and coat well. Cover, refrigerate and leave to marinate for at least 30 minutes.

3 Thread prawns through sugar cane skewers. Heat a grill pan over medium-high heat and brush lightly with oil. Place prawns onto pan and grill for 5–8 minutes on each side, or until prawns are cooked.

4 Arrange prawns and lettuce leaves on a serving plate. Serve immediately.

stir-fried squid with chilli paste
sambal sotong

When dressed up in a spicy, smoky homemade sambal, squid becomes an excellent dish that goes wonderfully with plain steamed rice! **Serves 4**

Squid 500 g (1 lb 1¹/₂ oz)

Cooking oil 2 Tbsp

Dried prawn (shrimp) paste (belacan)
1¹/₂ tsp

Red onion 1, peeled and diced

Sambal *belacan* **(see page 113)** 4 Tbsp

Brown sugar 1¹/₂ tsp

Tomatoes 2, finely chopped

Spring onion (scallion) 1, cut into
short lengths

1 Separate squid heads from bodies. Rinse tubes and set aside. Clean squid tubes by removing innards. Trim away fins at tail end. Cut open squid tubes. Pull away skin from inside of squid tube and discard.

2 Turn squid tubes over and remove the purplish skin. Cut squid into 8-cm (3-in) long pieces, then make criss-cross cuts on outside of squid tubes.

3 Heat oil in a large frying pan over medium heat, add dried prawn paste and red onion and stir-fry for 2 minutes, or until fragrant.

4 Add sambal *belacan*, brown sugar and tomatoes. Increase heat and stir-fry for 5 minutes or until sugar is completely dissolved and tomatoes break down into pulp. Reduce heat to low and leave to simmer until sauce is reduced to a thick consistency.

5 Add squid and stir-fry for about 4 minutes or until it is cooked.

6 Dish out, garnish with spring onion and serve immediately.

creamy miso seafood claypot stew
seafood nabemono

This Japanese claypot dish features a selection of fresh seafood stewed in a creamy, miso-laced broth. **Serves 4**

Clams 400 g (14^1/$_3$ oz)

Mussels 8–12

Squid 200 g (7 oz)

Cooking oil 2 Tbsp

Onion 1, peeled and thinly sliced

Garlic 4 cloves, peeled and finely chopped

Miso paste 1^1/$_2$ Tbsp

Dashi stock (see page 112)
200 ml (6^1/$_2$ fl oz)

Corn flour (cornstarch) 1 Tbsp, mixed with 1 Tbsp water

Prawns (shrimps) 200 g (7 oz), peeled and deveined, leaving tails intact

Chinese leeks 2 stalks, green portion trimmed, thinly sliced

Heavy cream 200 ml (6^1/$_2$ fl oz)

1 Soak clams and mussels together in a large container of water. Leave for about 30 minutes, drain and rinse in water again.

2 Pull off the beard found at the opening where both shells meet. Do this by pulling the beard towards the hinge of the mussel. Scrub mussels clean under running water, drain and set aside.

3 Clean squid (see page 88). Cut squid into small pieces, then make criss-cross cuts on the outside of squid tubes.

4 Heat oil in claypot over medium heat. Stir-fry onion and garlic until fragrant. Add miso paste, dashi stock and corn flour mixture. Stir to mix well, then increase heat and bring to a boil.

5 Add clams, mussels and prawns. Cover claypot with a lid and cook over high heat for 5 minutes. Add squid and leeks, then return cover and boil for another 3 minutes. Stir in cream and mix well.

6 Remove from heat and set aside. Uncover just before serving.

desserts

glutinous rice balls in sweet potato soup (china) 94

milk and pistachio ice cream (india) 97

apple fritters with caramel floss (china) 98

red bean pancake (korea) 101

lychee and lemon grass granita (vietnam) 102

fruit and shell pasta cocktail (the philippines) 105

sugee cupcakes (singapore) 106

sago ring with caramelised bananas (malaysia) 109

glutinous rice balls in sweet potato soup
tang yuan

Glutinous rice balls in a sweet soup are a favourite festive Chinese dish. The rice balls are made without flavouring, as they absorb the flavour of the sweet potato and ginger.
Serves 4

Glutinous rice flour 200 g (7 oz)

Rice flour 2 Tbsp

Water 160–180 ml (5-6 fl oz)

Ginger soup

Mature ginger 1 knob, 6-cm (2½-in)

Water 1.5 litres (48 fl oz / 6 cups)

Screwpine (*pandan*) leaves 4, knotted

Orange or brown sugar 85 g (3 oz)

Sweet potatoes 350 g (12 oz), peeled and cut into large chunks

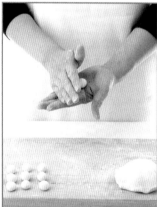

1 Use the back of a knife to hit or bruise ginger a couple of times.

2 Combine ingredients for ginger soup in a pot. Bring to the boil over high heat, then reduce heat to low. Leave mixture to simmer gently for 15–20 minutes, or until sweet potatoes are tender. Remove from heat and discard screwpine leaves and ginger. Set aside.

3 Combine both types of flour in a large mixing bowl. Gradually add water while kneading for about 3 minutes to get a smooth dough that leaves the sides of the bowl.

4 Roll dough into small balls and place on a lightly floured surface. Return sweet potato soup to the boil. Add rice balls and cook for about 5 minutes, or until rice balls float to the surface.

5 Pour into serving bowls. Serve warm.

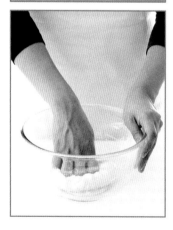

milk and pistachio ice cream kulfi

Sweet and creamy, with the nutty undertones of pistachio and cloves, this traditional Indian dessert will be a great treat to have on a hot day. If tin kulfi moulds are not available, use popsicle moulds or ice cube trays. Serves 4

Pistachio nuts 25 g (1 oz)

Full cream milk 500 ml (16 fl oz / 2 cups)

Evaporated milk 250 ml (8 fl oz / 1 cup)

Sugar 3 Tbsp

Sweetened condensed milk 1 Tbsp

Cloves 6

Ice cubes and iced water

1 Chop pistachio nuts up coarsely and set aside.

2 Place all ingredients except pistachio nuts in a small pot and bring to the boil over medium heat. Reduce heat and simmer for 25–30 minutes until milk is reduced to about a third of the original volume and has a slightly thick consistency.

3 Place ice cubes and iced water in a large basin. Remove pot from stove and place in basin. Incorporate pistachio nuts by stirring into mixture. When mixture has cooled, pour into kulfi moulds, popsicle moulds or into an ice cube tray. Freeze overnight for kulfi to set.

4 To serve, unmould kulfi by dipping moulds in a bowl of warm water for a few seconds. Serve immediately.

Note: For a healthier version, use low-fat, high-calcium milk.

apple fritters with caramel floss
ping guo chui

Crisp and hot, these tasty apple fritters with a golden caramel floss are truly a treat too good to pass up! Chose tart apples for best results. Serves 4–6

Cooking oil for deep-frying

Green apples 4, pared, cored and cut into wedges

Batter

Plain (all-purpose) flour 75 g (2¹/₃ oz)

Rice flour 100 g (3¹/₂ oz)

Baking powder 1 tsp

Ground cinnamon ¹/₄ tsp

Castor (superfine) sugar 1 tsp

Salt ¹/₄ tsp

Cold water 250 ml (8 fl oz / 1 cup)

Caramel floss

Sugar 150 g (5¹/₃ oz)

Water 150 ml (5 fl oz / 1³/₄ cups)

1 Prepare batter. Sift plain flour, rice flour, baking powder and ground cinnamon into a large mixing bowl. Add sugar and salt. Mix well. Gradually add cold water, stirring to form a smooth batter.

2 Heat oil for deep-frying in a large frying pan.

3 Dip apples in batter, then gently lower, one at a time, into hot oil to prevent sticking. Fry for 3–5 minutes or until golden brown. Remove from pan and place on paper towels to drain.

4 Prepare caramel floss. Place sugar and water in a small saucepan and bring to a rolling boil. When mixture turns light golden brown in colour, remove from heat and let it develop a golden caramel hue. If this does not happen, reheat for another few minutes. Do not stir mixture at any point.

5 Place apple fritters on a serving plate. Dip a fork into caramel and 'spin' it around on top of apple fritters until a fine caramel thread appears. Serve immediately.

Note: Do not stir sugar syrup when making caramel. Be extra careful when boiling caramel as it has a temperature much higher than boiling water. Do not touch caramel with bare hands. Hardened caramel can be removed from the pot by filling the pot three-quarters full with water, then bringing it to the boil for 5–10 minutes.

red bean pancake pot jun

This traditional Korean snack features red bean paste wrapped in a thin crêpe. Serves 4

Store-bought Korean or Japanese
   red bean paste 300 g (11 oz)

Cooking oil as needed

Batter

Plain (all-purpose) flour 100 g (3¹/₂ oz),
   sifted

Milk 280 ml (9¹/₂ fl oz)

Salt a pinch

Egg 1

Egg yolk 1

Unsalted butter 30 g (1 oz), melted

1 Place red bean paste in a pot and gently heat over low-medium heat for 3–5 minutes. Stir gently to ensure paste heats evenly, then remove from heat and set aside.

2 Prepare batter. Combine flour, milk, salt and eggs in a large mixing bowl and whisk until smooth.

3 Coat a small non-stick frying pan with a little oil, then pour a ladleful of batter into the pan. Swirl pan around so batter coats base of pan. Leave to cook for about 2 minutes on both sides, until crêpe is light brown. Repeat to make more crêpes until batter is used up.

4 Place a crêpe on a flat work surface, then place with a heaped tablespoonful of red bean paste onto the centre of crêpe. Fold 2 opposite sides of crêpe over red bean paste, then fold open ends over to form a parcel. Repeat until ingredients are used up.

Note: For a more nutritious version, use low-fat, high-calcium milk.

lychee and lemon grass granita
qua vai kem

A sweet marriage of lychee and aromatic lemon grass in the form of a granita is the perfect answer for cooling off on a swelteringly hot day. Serves 4

Canned lychees 500 g (1 lb 1^1/$_2$ oz), seeded

Lemon grass 2 stalks, tough outer layers
    removed and bruised

Lychee syrup (from can)
    350 ml (11^4/$_5$ fl oz)

Water 500 ml (16 fl oz / 2 cups)

Lime ^{1}/$_2$, squeezed for juice and
    grated for zest

Sugar 150 g (5^1/$_3$ oz)

1   Place lychees is a blender and blend into a purée. Set aside.

2   Combine lemon grass, lychee syrup, water, lime juice, zest and sugar in a large pot and bring to the boil over high heat. Add lychee purée and stir to mix well. Bring mixture to a gentle boil for about 3 minutes. Discard lemon grass stalks, then remove from heat and set aside to cool.

3   Pour cooled lychee mixture into a shallow, freezer-proof container. Cover and freeze for 1 hour. Using a fork, scrape to break up the ice crystals. Repeat this procedure twice every 45–50 minutes to ensure the formation of small, fine ice crystals for the granita.

4   To serve, use a spoon or fork to scrape granita crystals. Put in serving glasses. Garnish as desired and serve immediately.

fruit and shell pasta cocktail

This unlikely combination of fruit medley mixed with mini shell pasta dressed in mayonnaise and condensed milk is a party favourite, especially with children. Serves 4

Shell pasta 300 g (11 oz)

Condensed milk 3 Tbsp

Canned peaches 55 g (2 oz), cut into cubes

Pear 55 g (2 oz), cored and cut into cubes

Canned nata de coco 55 g (2 oz)

Maraschino cherries 5, cut into halves

Raisins 30 g (1 oz)

Mayonnaise 4 Tbsp

1   Bring a pot of water to the boil and cook pasta for 10–12 minutes until al dente. Drain and rinse with cold water, then drain again.

2   Place pasta into a large mixing bowl. Add condensed milk and mix well. Refrigerate for 45 minutes to chill.

3   Add remaining ingredients to chilled pasta and mix well. Refrigerate until ready to serve.

sugee cupcakes

This classic Eurasian cake is perfect for breakfast or tea-time, and goes well with tea or coffee. Makes two 18-cm (7-in) loaves or 12 cupcakes

Eggs 4

Orange juice 3 Tbsp

Orange zest 2 tsp

Semolina 150 g (5$^{1}/_{3}$ oz)

Unsalted butter 280 g (10 oz),
  at room temperature

Castor (superfine) sugar 150 g (5$^{1}/_{3}$ oz)

Egg yolks 4

Cake flour 110 g (4 oz), sifted

Baking powder $^{1}/_{4}$ tsp, sifted

Dried apricots 40 g (1$^{1}/_{2}$ oz), thinly sliced

Dried pitted prunes 40 g (1$^{1}/_{2}$ oz),
  thinly sliced

1. Preheat oven to 170°C (330°F). Line two 18-cm (7-in) loaf tins, or line muffin tray with cupcake holders.

2. Beat eggs and orange juice in a mixing bowl. Add semolina and leave to soak for 1 hour.

3. Place butter and sugar in a mixing bowl, then cream using an using an electric cake mixer. Beat until mixture is white and fluffy. Add egg yolks one at a time, making sure each yolk is well incorporated before adding the next.

4. Remove mixing bowl from cake mixer. Gently fold in semolina mixture. Place flour and baking powder into a bowl and stir in mixed fruit. Fold mixture into butter and semolina mixture until just incorporated.

5. Pour batter into loaf tins or muffin cups until 2-cm (1-in) from the rim. Bake for 40–50 minutes until golden if using a loaf tin, and 25–35 minutes if using muffin cups. Remove from heat and set on a wire rack to cool before serving. If not consuming immediately, wrap cake loaves with cling wrap or store cupcakes in airtight containers for up to 3 days.

Note: Make sure ingredients are at room temperature to achieve the best results for the creaming method.

sago ring with caramelised bananas
sago gula melaka

Sago has little taste on its own, so it is perfect when served with a little palm sugar and coconut milk. Top with caramelised bananas for a special treat! **Serves 4**

Water 1.5 litres (48 fl oz / 6 cups)

Pearl sago 200 g (7 oz), rinsed and drained

Cooking oil 1 Tbsp

Large bananas 3, peeled and sliced

Brown sugar 1¹/₂ Tbsp

Coconut milk 4 Tbsp

Sugar syrup

Palm sugar 150 g (5¹/₃ oz)

Water 150 ml (5 fl oz)

1. Bring water to the boil in a large pot. While stirring, gradually add sago pearls. Cook for about 10 minutes, or until sago is translucent. Pour sago through a fine strainer, then rinse with running water for a few minutes to remove excess starch. Sago pearls should look clear and not opaque.

2. Spoon sago into pudding or jelly moulds and place in the refrigerator to cool for at least 5 hours or overnight.

3. Prepare syrup. Using a knife, cut palm sugar coarsely. Place palm sugar and water in a saucepan and simmer until sugar is dissolved and has a thickened consistency. Strain, then set aside to cool.

4. Heat oil on non-stick frying pan. Coat bananas with a little brown sugar and pan-fry for 1–2 minutes until slightly brown. Remove from pan and set aside.

5. To serve, remove sago from mould and place on individual serving plates. Pour 1 Tbsp each of sugar syrup and coconut milk over pudding and top with caramelised bananas.

Note: Handle sago with wet hands to prevent sticking.

basic recipes

dashi stock

Makes about 1 litre (40 fl oz / 4 cups)

Kelp (*kombu*) 30 g (1 oz), or 1 postcard size

Bonito flakes 10 g ($^1/_3$ oz)

Water 1 litre (32 fl oz / 4 cups)

1 Combine kelp and water in a pot and bring to boil on medium heat. Leave to boil for 30 minutes.

2 Remove kombu, then add bonito flakes. Return stock to the boil for 10 minutes. Remove from heat and strain before use.

3 If not using immediately, leave stock to cool, then refrigerate for up to 3 days.

chicken stock

Makes about 2 litres (64 fl oz / 8 cups)

Water 2 litres (64 fl oz / 8 cups)

Whole chicken 1. or 500 g (1 lb 1$^1/_2$ oz) chicken bones

Brown onion 1, peeled

Garlic 4 cloves

Spring onions (scallions) 2

1 Combine all ingredients in a large pot and bring to boil over medium heat.

2 When mixture boils, reduce heat to low. Leave to simmer for about 1 hour.

3 Remove from heat and strain before use. If not using immediately, store in an airtight container up to 3 days, or freeze for up to 1 month.

seafood stock

Makes about 1.5 litres (48 fl oz / 6 cups)

Water 1.5 litres (48 fl oz / 6 cups)

Fish head and bones 300 g (11 oz)

Prawn heads and shells 300 g (11 oz)

Ginger 3 slices

Brown onion 1, peeled

Salt 1 tsp

1 Combine all ingredients in a large pot and bring to boil over medium heat.

2 When mixture boils, reduce heat to low. Leave to simmer for about 40 minutes to 1 hour.

3 Remove from heat and strain before use. If not using immediately, store in an airtight container 3 days, or freeze for up to 1 month.

red curry paste

Yield about 125 g (4½ oz)

Large dried red chillies 5, soaked in warm water until soft and seeded

Lemon grass 2 stalks, hard outer leaves removed, ends trimmed and sliced

Shallots 10, peeled and sliced

Garlic 10 cloves, peeled and sliced

Galangal 1 thin slice

Coriander (cilantro) root 3

Prawn (shrimp) paste (*belacan*) 1 tsp

Kaffir lime leaves 3, centre vein removed and thinly sliced

Kaffir lime 1, grated for zest

Brown sugar ½ tsp

Ground black pepper ¼ tsp

1 Combine all ingredients in a blender and blend into a fine paste.

2 If not using immediately, store paste in an airtight container. Refrigerate for up to 2 days, or freeze for up to 1 month.

sambal belacan

Yields about 85 g (3 oz)

Red chillies 8, seeded and sliced

Shallots 6, peeled and sliced

Garlic 4 cloves, peeled and sliced

Ginger 1 thin slice

Dried prawns (shrimp) 1 Tbsp

Canola oil 2 Tbsp

Cooking oil 3 Tbsp

Prawn (shrimp) paste (*belacan*) 2 tsp

Brown sugar 1½ tsp

1 Combine chillies, shallots, garlic, ginger, dried prawns and canola oil in a blender and blend into a fine paste. Set aside.

2 Heat cooking oil in a frying pan over medium heat. Stir-fry prawn paste for 1–2 minutes, or until fragrant. Add sugar and spice paste and stir-fry for 15-30 minutes, or until paste is deep red in colour.

3 If not using immediately, store sambal *belacan* in an airtight container. Refrigerate for up to 2 days, or freeze for up to 1 month.

glossary

1. Basil
Basil is an aromatic herb that has many varieties. In this book, Thai or sweet basili is used. It has a sweet, peppery aroma, purplish stems and a flavour similar to that of anise.

2. Deep-fried bean curd pockets
This thin, rectangular-shaped bean curd is high versatile, and can be added to many dishes including stir-fries, simmered dishes and soups. Rich in vegetable protein, it can also be used like a pocket, for stuffing with sushi rice and vegetables.

3. Prawn (shrimp) paste (*belacan*)
Prawn paste, or *belacan* as it is known in Malay, is a pungent, strong-smelling condiment that is used to flavour sauces and dishes. Before use, it is either grilled or roasted to neutralise its fishy flavour. Roasted prawn paste can be stored for several months in airtight containers. Although pungent, prawn paste adds an appetising and pleasant flavour when used in dishes.

4. Dried Chinese mushrooms
Dried Chinese mushrooms have an intensified flavour due to the drying process. They should be reconstituted in water before use.

5. Dried Chinese sausages
"Chinese sausage" is generic term to describe the different types of sausages that the Chinese make. They are usually made of beef or pork. Some varieties are made from liver. Chinese sausages are sold in dried form, and have a sweet-salty taste.

6. Dried Thai stick noodles
Dried Thai stick noodles are commonly used for stir-fried noodle dishes, and characterise the classic *pad thai*. Reconstitute to soften in water before use.

7. Galangal

Galangal is a rhizome belonging to the same family as ginger. Its colour ranges from ivory to pale yellow, with pink-tinged tips at the ends of its bulbous stems. It has a sharp, slightly citrusy flavour, which adds a refreshing zing to dishes.

8. Garlic chives

With long, slender green leaves and a flavour that resembles garlic, garlic chives are also known as Chinese chives, and have a much stronger flavour as compared to their Western counterpart. Choose bunches that are have unblemished leaves and firm, shiny green stems.

9. Gingko nuts

Gingko nuts are commonly used in Chinese desserts. When peeled, they are a pale, creamy yellow colour, with a smooth texture. Their flavour is distinctively buttery and bitter-sweet. The bitter shoot located in the core of the nuts should be removed before use.

10. Ginseng

Ginseng is a highly prized ingredient in the realm of Chinese cuisine. Aromatic, with a slightly bitter, medicinal taste, the Chinese believe that is has restorative properties to heal and invigorate the body. Each variety of ginseng has several grades according to quality. Ginseng is usually added to soups for flavour and nutrition, and is available in fresh and dried form.

11. Nameko mushrooms

Also known as butterscotch mushrooms because of their rich brown hue, nameko mushrooms are commonly used in soups and stews in Japanese cooking.

12. Wood ear fungus

Black and crinkled, wood ear fungus is also known as Jew's ears or black fungus. Dried wood ear fungus expands considerably when reconstituted in water. It should be soaked until soft and jelly-like, and hard gritty bits should be cut away. It is also sold fresh.

13. Kaffir lime leaves

Easily recognisable by their dual leaves shape, kaffir lime leaves are used lavishly in Thai cooking. Even when used sparingly, kaffir lime leaves impart a flavour that cannot easily be replicated by any other citrus leaf substitute.

115

14. Korean chilli paste

Known as *gochujang*, Korean chilli paste has a wide variety of uses in Korean cooking. It can be served as a condiment, used as a base for stews, and as a marinade for meats.

15. Lemon grass

Lemon grass is a highly aromatic herb with long, slender leaves and bulbous stems. The stems contain glands that release pungent oils when sliced or bruised, which impart a distinctive, lemony flavour to the dish it is added to.

16. Palm sugar (*gula melaka*)

Made from the sap of the coconut palm, palm sugar is sold either as solid blocks or slabs. Thai palm sugar tends to be light brown, with beige hues, whereas Indonesian or Malaysian varieties tend to be much darker in colour. Store away from heat and direct sunlight in an airtight container for a longer shelf life.

17. Screwpine (*pandan*) leaves

Screwpine leaves lend a wonderful aroma and subtle floral flavour to steamed rice, meat dishes and desserts. Fresh screwpine leaves should be a dark, shiny green colour, with a stiff spine.

18. Vietnamese rice paper

Vietnamese rice paper is made from water and rice flour. It is translucent and thin, and should be briefly soaked in water to soften slightly before use.

19. White (distilled) vinegar

White or distilled vinegar is comparatively milder and less acidic as compared to the variety of white vinegar made from grains or alcohol. It is used to add a piquant flavour to dishes.

20. Rose apple (*jambu*)

Smooth and shiny, with a waxy feel to its skin, rose apples or have a crunchy texture and juicy flesh. It has a faint, slightly acidic flavour, which makes it suitable to be used in salads and to pair with sweet or spicy dipping sauces as a snack.

21. Sago pearls

Sago pearls are made from the starch of the sago palm. In the preparation process, the starch is washed in water, strained through a

22

23

24

25

26

27

sieve and dried on a hot surface. When cooked, sago pearls turn translucent and sticky, and can be used to make desserts or shells for savoury fillings.

22. Seaweed (*nori*)

Nori seaweed is sold dried. It has a dark, greenish-brown hue, with a smoky flavour. It is commonly used for wrapping sushi rice and in soups. To obtain a crisp texture and accentuate its aroma, toast *nori* lightly before use.

23. Semolina

Semolina is the hard endosperm that is sifted out of durum wheat. It is granular, and available in a fine, medium-fine and coarse grind. It can be used in savoury dishes, such as couscous, and to make sweet cakes and pastries.

24. Sugar cane

Sugar cane is primarily cultivated for white (refined) sugar. It has proven useful as skewers for grilled meats and seafood, and in some parts of Asia, it is also squeezed for its juice which is consumed as a sweet, refreshing drink.

25. Tamarind

Tamarind is characterised by its dark brown, moist, sticky flesh. Its sweet-sourish taste is a common feature in many Thai dishes. Tamarind is sold in its pod, or in block form.

26. Turmeric

Also known as yellow ginger or *kunyit* in Malay, turmeric is a member of the ginger family. The orange-brown rhizomes are peeled before use. Turmeric is also available in powdered form.

27. Udon

Udon is a type of thick Japanese noodle made from wheat. They are typically served in a clear broth. In Japan, they are served chilled in the summer and hot in winter. Udon noodles are sold fresh in many supermarkets.

weights and measures

Quantities for this book are given in Metric, Imperial and American (spoon) measures. Standard spoon and cup measurements used are: 1 tsp = 5 ml, 1 Tbsp = 15 ml, 1 cup = 250 ml. All measures are level unless otherwise stated.

LIQUID AND VOLUME MEASURES

Metric	Imperial	American
5 ml	$^1/_6$ fl oz	1 teaspoon
10 ml	$^1/_3$ fl oz	1 dessertspoon
15 ml	$^1/_2$ fl oz	1 tablespoon
60 ml	2 fl oz	$^1/_4$ cup (4 tablespoons)
85 ml	$2^1/_2$ fl oz	$^1/_3$ cup
90 ml	3 fl oz	$^3/_8$ cup (6 tablespoons)
125 ml	4 fl oz	$^1/_2$ cup
180 ml	6 fl oz	$^3/_4$ cup
250 ml	8 fl oz	1 cup
300 ml	10 fl oz ($^1/_2$ pint)	$1^1/_4$ cups
375 ml	12 fl oz	$1^1/_2$ cups
435 ml	14 fl oz	$1^3/_4$ cups
500 ml	16 fl oz	2 cups
625 ml	20 fl oz (1 pint)	$2^1/_2$ cups
750 ml	24 fl oz ($1^1/_5$ pints)	3 cups
1 litre	32 fl oz ($1^3/_5$ pints)	4 cups
1.25 litres	40 fl oz (2 pints)	5 cups
1.5 litres	48 fl oz ($2^2/_5$ pints)	6 cups
2.5 litres	80 fl oz (4 pints)	10 cups

DRY MEASURES

Metric	Imperial
30 grams	1 ounce
45 grams	$1^1/_2$ ounces
55 grams	2 ounces
70 grams	$2^1/_2$ ounces
85 grams	3 ounces
100 grams	$3^1/_2$ ounces
110 grams	4 ounces
125 grams	$4^1/_2$ ounces
140 grams	5 ounces
280 grams	10 ounces
450 grams	16 ounces (1 pound)
500 grams	1 pound, $1^1/_2$ ounces
700 grams	$1^1/_2$ pounds
800 grams	$1^3/_4$ pounds
1 kilogram	2 pounds, 3 ounces
1.5 kilograms	3 pounds, $4^1/_2$ ounces
2 kilograms	4 pounds, 6 ounces

OVEN TEMPERATURE

	°C	°F	Gas Regulo
Very slow	120	250	1
Slow	150	300	2
Moderately slow	160	325	3
Moderate	180	350	4
Moderately hot	190/200	370/400	5/6
Hot	210/220	410/440	6/7
Very hot	230	450	8
Super hot	250/290	475/550	9/10

LENGTH

Metric	Imperial
0.5 cm	$^1/_4$ inch
1 cm	$^1/_2$ inch
1.5 cm	$^3/_4$ inch
2.5 cm	1 inch

index